Jams, Jellies & Preserves

Jams, Jellies & Preserves

Make Beautiful Gifts to Give (or Keep)

LINDA FERRARI

PRIMA PUBLISHING

PRIMA PUBLISHING, its colophon, and GOOD GIFTS FROM THE HOME are trademarks of Prima Publishing, a division of Prima Communications, Inc.

DISCLAIMER: THE EXPRESS PURPOSE OF *JAMS, JELLIES & PRESERVES* IS TO PROVIDE SUGGESTIONS FOR A RECREATIONAL HOBBY. THE AUTHOR AND PUBLISHER DISCLAIM ANY WARRANTY OR GUARANTEE, EXPRESS OR IMPLIED, FOR ANY OF THE RECIPES OR FORMULAS CONTAINED HEREIN AND FURTHER DISCLAIM ANY LIABILITY FOR THE READER'S EXPERIMENTS OR PROJECTS. THE AUTHOR OR PUBLISHER DO NOT ASSUME ANY LIABILITY FOR ANY DAMAGES THAT MAY OCCUR AS A RESULT OF READING OR FOLLOWING ANY OF THE RECIPES OR FORMULAS IN THIS BOOK. THE PURCHASE OF THIS BOOK BY THE READER WILL SERVE AS AN ACKNOWLEDGMENT OF THIS DISCLAIMER AND AN AGREEMENT TO HOLD THE AUTHOR AND PUBLISHER HARMLESS FOR ANY MISTAKES THE READER MAY MAKE AS A RESULT OF FOLLOWING THE RECIPES AND FORMULAS IN THIS BOOK.

Library of Congress Cataloging-in-Publication Data

Ferrari, Linda.
   Jams, jellies & preserves / by Linda Ferrari.
      p.   cm. — (Good gifts from the home)

   Includes index.
   ISBN 0-7615-0332-3
   1. Jam.   2. Jelly.   3. Fruit—Preservation.   I. Title.
II. Series.
TX612.J3F47 1996   95-26068
641.8'52—dc20   CIP

96 97 98 99 00 AA 10 9 8 7 6 5 4 3 2 1

Printed in the United States of America

How to Order:

Single copies may be ordered from Prima Publishing, P.O. Box 1260BK, Rocklin, CA 95677; telephone (916) 632-4400. Quantity discounts are also available. On your letterhead, include information concerning the intended use of the books and the number of books you wish to purchase.

❏ To the shining stars in my life:

Philip, Michelle, Cindy, Suzy, Carrie, and T.J.

CONTENTS

ACKNOWLEDGMENTS

THANKS TO everyone involved in this series at Prima Publishing. I acknowledge Jennifer Basye Sander for being the first to bring this idea to my attention, and for always lending an ear when needed. Special thanks are due to Alice Anderson for working on these ideas with me, and to Leslie Yarborough for overseeing the completion of the book. I appreciate the efforts of the Dunlavey Studio for the cover, and Jaime Robles for the interior design. I also recognize Archetype Book Composition for the layout and final composition of the work. As always, I am grateful to my agent Linda Hayes, who keeps me humming.

. . . .

回 WITH THE fierce and frenzied lives so many of us find ourselves living today, it is no wonder that we, with the images of our grandmothers before us, are determined to rekindle the spirit of early American life. We each have our own way of accomplishing this—some through quilting, rug making, country wood and flower crafts, bread making, or perhaps preserving, to name just a few.

In this volume of the Good Gifts from the Home you will learn to make some fantastic jams, jellies, and preserves. Our modern supermarkets and impressive farmers' markets now provide us with some truly gorgeous fruits and vegetables. Rather than just picking a bowl of berries and making a jam (which is still exquisite), you can now mix and match fruits and vegetables to create some intriguing combinations that will bring to mind marvelous images of summer all year long. These jams, jellies, and preserves also make wonderful gifts to give to friends and relatives. Everyone loves a gift that you have taken time and effort to prepare.

How-Tos of Making Jams, Jellies, and Preserves

Making jams, jellies, and preserves is very quick and easy to do. For most, the greatest difficulty is in getting started. I hope you've overcome any initial doubts and gained confidence just by purchasing this book. Remember—you don't have to start out making hundreds of jars of preserves. Begin with just a few beautiful jars that will bring you great enjoyment.

. . . .

Choosing the Perfect Fruit

When preserving, make sure that the fruit you use is perfectly ripe. Using under-ripe or overripe fruit will produce an inferior product that may not jell properly. If fruit is too ripe it loses its natural acid and what pectin the fruit may contain. These components of fresh ripe fruit, sugar, acid, and pectin all come together to produce the perfect jelled fruit.

In addition, each of these recipes contains instructions for all necessary peeling, pitting, chopping, and mashing to produce a perfect jam, jelly, or preserve.

Deciding Whether to "Short-Boil" or "Long-Boil"

Two methods of cooking are used in these recipes: the *short-boil* method requires the use of a commercially bought pectin as a jelling agent. This additional pectin simply speeds up the process. The *long-boil* method does not require the addition of pectin because the combination of naturally occurring pectin, sugar, and acid along with a longer cooking time causes the mixture to reach jell point. The jell point is usually 220°F at sea level for a firm jell or 218°F for a softer jell.

Most of these recipes use the short-boil method, and require the addition of either dry or liquid pectin (for best results, use liquid pectin when I suggest it). Please follow carefully the directions given on the boxes of dry or liquid pectin. Also, when using the short-boil method, be sure to add the recommended amount of sugar and citric acid to ensure proper jelling. You will enjoy a higher success rate if you follow the recipes as closely as possible.

If you are looking to cut the amount of sugar in a recipe, use the long-boil method; you'll have greater control over the jelling process.

🔲 *When using less sugar, preserves, jams, and jellies will have to cook a little longer, but the results will be the same.*

When Is It Done?

Any of the following methods will ensure your jams, jellies, or preserves reach the jell point:

Utilize a commercially made pectin   A commercially made pectin will provide consistent results if you follow the directions on the package precisely.

Use a candy thermometer   When your candy thermometer reads 218–220°F, simply remove the jam, jelly, or preserve from the heat.

The sheeting method   My favorite way—it takes a little practice—is the sheeting method. To use this technique, cool a large metal spoon in the refrigerator. Dip the cold spoon into the boiling jelly and lift the spoon high enough to be out of the pot's "steam zone"; then turn the spoon sideways and let the jelly run off. If the jelly drips off or is syrupy it is not done. When it drops off and two drops flow together it is done.

The plate test   Refrigerate a small plate until it is well chilled. Place a little of the hot jam, jelly, or preserve on the plate. Put the plate with its sample in the freezer for a minute, then test the mixture with your finger. It should hold its shape when touched and not have watery edges.

Equipment: Be Prepared

You won't need much in the way of special equipment to make jams, jellies, and preserves. Before beginning, check that the following items are at hand:

- Chopper, food processor, food mill, or grinder
- 5-quart pot, heavyweight pan, oven-proof pan, Dutch oven, or jelly pan
- Jelly bag or strainer lined with cheesecloth, colander
- Miscellaneous: Candy thermometer, paper towels, timer, measuring spoons and cups, hot damp cloths, heavy spoon or potato masher
- Jars, jar lifter, wide-mouth canning funnel
- Hot water bath for final processing

About the pot or pan you use: I recommend a heavy-weight pan that is large enough for the jelly to boil in, or a lovely unlined copper jelly pan.

You'll need the cheesecloth-lined strainer or jelly bag to hold crushed fruit while it's releasing its juices. You can first crush the fruit with a large spoon, potato masher, or food processor.

Some extra notes about jars: I recommend using the traditional jars with the two-piece lids that are sold everywhere. These jars are made of tempered glass and will withstand changing temperatures without cracking or breaking. Other decorative jars can be used, but you must be very careful that you have a proper seal so the food won't spoil. If you are using jars with rubber rings, make sure you always start with a new rim; these also are readily available.

The last piece of equipment I want to talk about is the water bath canner. A water bath canner is used for fruit, tomatoes, fruit butters, preserves, pickles, relishes, chutneys, or any foods high in acid. You can find these large, black-spotted canners in almost any grocery or hardware store. They come with a wire rack that holds up to seven quart-size jars at a time. They are inexpensive and indispensable, if you plan on doing much canning. I recommend putting your jars of jams, jellies, and preserves into a water bath canner for 5 to 10 minutes to ensure a good seal. I am sure many of you are remembering that your grandmothers and mothers never did any more than put very hot jam into a very hot jar, seal it with a lid or paraffin, and put it on a towel until they heard the sweet-sounding "pop" of the lid to know the jam sealed. My mom used to say, "Do you hear those jars singing?" when we heard the lids pop. It is true that if everything is very hot you probably don't need to process the preserves in a water bath. But because we are concerned with safety, it is a very good precaution.

After the jars have cooled, check the lids—they should be slightly concave in appearance. When pressed slightly, the lids should make no sound. If for any reason your jams, jellies, or preserves have not sealed you should reprocess them in the water bath by removing the lids, cleaning the rims of the jars with hot cloths, resealing with new hot lids, and putting the sealed jars in the water bath for 10 more minutes. If time does not permit you to reseal the jars, just refrigerate them until needed.

Summary of Steps for Successful Jams, Jellies, and Preserves

1. Have all your equipment ready before you start. Make your job easy by having a pan to keep jars warm, a water bath canner, a colander, a funnel, a jar lifter, ladles, measuring cups, and thermometers all clean and ready to go before starting.
2. Sterilize the proper number of jars and keep them hot until ready to use. Jars can be sterilized in pans of boiling water or in your dishwasher.
3. Wash, pit, peel, chop, or mash the fruit as instructed in the recipe. Great pitters and corers are available for apples, pears, peaches, plums, nectarines,

and cherries to make your job fast and easy. Fruits can be chopped or mashed with a knife, food processor, grinder, or food mill.

4. Strain the fruit for juice, if making jelly: mash the fruit by hand or in a food processor, or heat the fruit until it softens and then let the juice strain from a suspended jelly bag or a strainer lined with several layers of dampened cheesecloth. Juice may be used immediately or frozen for making jelly at a more convenient time.

5. Cook the fruit according to the directions in the recipe. When using pectin, read the package directions also.

6. Follow the recipe precisely unless the recipe states that amounts can fluctuate. It is important to follow directions to achieve proper jelling.

7. When the mixture reaches the jelling point, remove the pan from the heat. The jelling point is determined by use of a candy thermometer (218–220°F), or by using one of the other methods described earlier.

8. Skim off any accumulated foam from the top of the jam, jelly, or preserves. Foam that is not removed looks unsightly when the jar is opened.

9. If making preserves or jams, let the mixture sit for 5 minutes before ladling into jars. Letting the mixture rest keeps the fruit from floating to the top of the jar when cooling.

10. Leave ½ inch of headspace at the top of each jar. This prevents the jam from touching the lid of the jar and darkening in color.

11. Clean the rim of each jar with a clean, hot, damp cloth (we do not want any bacteria to form).

12. Place a hot lid on each jar and screw on the metal band. Heating the lid makes it seal more easily.

13. Put the jars of jam, jelly, or preserves in a boiling water bath for 5 to 10 minutes. This will assure you of a tight seal.

14. Remove the jars and put them on a folded towel or wooden cutting board to cool. If the jars are put onto a cold surface such as a tile countertop, they will probably crack and break.

15. Listen for the popping sound of your jars. This lets you know that the lids have "pulled down" and sealed.

16. In about 2 hours, check to see that all of the jars have popped and have slightly concave lids, and that the lids make no sounds when pressed. If the jars have not sealed, put them into the water bath again or store them in the refrigerator until ready to use.

17. Store your jams, jellies, and preserves in a dark, cool, dry place. This helps prevent the contents of the jars from darkening.

Common Problems with Preserving: Causes and Solutions ·

Jams or jellies too hard   If your jams or jellies are too hard, you have cooked them too long or used too much pectin—read the label of the pectin package carefully before starting and follow the recipe directions precisely.

Jams or jellies too soft   If your jams and jellies are too soft, you have probably not cooked them long enough; or you may not have used enough pectin or enough sugar with the pectin.

Cloudy jelly   If your jelly is cloudy you probably squeezed the jelly bag or did not strain the fruit juice carefully.

Crystallized sugar or tough-feeling fruit in preserves, jams, or jellies   If the sugar crystallizes in your preserves, or the fruit pieces feel tough, you have used too much sugar or cooked the mixture too long.

Fruit at top of jars   If fruit rises to the top of your jars of preserves, you probably didn't let the mixture rest for 5 minutes before ladling it into jars.

CHAPTER ONE

Jams

IT'S A VERY COZY feeling when the fragrance of jam, simmering on the stove, fills the house with the sweet smells of summer. Jam is a delicious spreadable condiment made of crushed or chopped fruit that is cooked to a thick, spreadable consistency. You can cook your jam on top of the stove or in a large pan in the oven, using either the *long-boil* method or the *short-boil* method (see page xii). Another way to make jam is called the "no-cook" method, and the jam produced is often referred to as *freezer jam.* You'll use pectin to make freezer jam, which has a superior fresh taste because it is never cooked. Freezer jam is best when defrosted in the refrigerator overnight, and has so many wonderful uses. I like using it in mousses to fill cakes, or mixed with sour cream and whipping cream for a fruit dip, or stirred into a favorite cheesecake. It's terrific!

. . . .

Reminiscent of my dad's all-time favorite pie, Apple–Rhubarb Jam is delicious on a big Dutch baby pancake.

Makes about 6 half-pints

> 4 cups peeled, cored, and chopped Granny Smith apples
> 2 cups diced rhubarb
> Zest of 1 lemon
> 2 tablespoons lemon juice
> 4 cups brown sugar
> 1 teaspoon cinnamon
> ½ teaspoon *each* nutmeg and mace
> 2 tablespoons rum

Put all of the ingredients, except the rum, into a heavy 5-quart pot, and bring to a boil. Stir until the sugar dissolves completely. Reduce the heat and cook to a temperature of 218–220°F, skimming off any foam as it cooks. Remove from heat, stir in the rum, and let the mixture sit for 5 minutes. Ladle into prepared jars and continue as described on pages xvii–xviii.

. . . .

CHERRY—AMARETTO JAM

....

I save the large Bing and Rainier cherries to brandy whole, and use our small varieties for jams and preserves.

Makes about 6 half-pints

> 3 cups pitted, chopped, and crushed sweet cherries
> 1 cup peeled, pits removed, chopped fresh peaches
> 2 tablespoons lemon juice
> One (1¾ ounce) package powdered pectin
> 5 cups sugar
> 3 tablespoons Amaretto

Place the fruit, lemon juice, and pectin into a large, heavy pot and bring the mixture to a rolling boil. Add the sugar all at once and bring the mixture back to a rolling boil (i.e., one that cannot be stirred down). Cook from this point for 1 minute exactly, stirring all the time. Remove from the stove and skim off any foam from the top of the mixture. Stir in the Amaretto. Let the jam sit for 5 minutes and then ladle it into jars as described on pages xvii–xviii.

....

. . . .

If you are lucky enough to get wild blueberries (they are tiny, like the ones that come in cans in commercial blueberry muffin mix), get as many as you can and freeze them. My grandmother would pick quarts of these berries and give them to my mother to freeze and use. I wish I knew someone with the patience to pick quarts for me.

Makes about 4 to 5 half-pints

> 1 quart blueberries, washed and picked over
> 3 cups sugar
> Juice of 2 lemons
> 2 tablespoons lemon zest
> 1 teaspoon cardamom
> 2 tablespoons Grand Marnier

Put the berries, sugar, lemon juice, zest, and cardamom into a heavyweight pan and bring the mixture to a boil. Stir constantly until the sugar dissolves. Reduce the heat to medium and continue to cook and stir until the mixture reaches 218–220°F, or until it is as thick as you like. Remove from heat and discard any accumulated foam from the jam. Let the mixture rest for 5 minutes and then ladle it into hot clean jars. Continue as described on pages xvii–xviii.

. . . .

APRICOT FREEZER JAM

. . . .

Freezer jam is the most beguiling of all jams, because the fresh-picked flavor of the fruit is retained. You can use any fruit you want for freezer jam—some good choices are peach, strawberry, blackberry, cherries, and raspberries.

Makes 7 half-pints

> 2 ½ cups chopped apricots
> 5 cups sugar
> ½ cup corn syrup
> 2 tablespoons lemon juice
> One (1 ¾ ounce) package powdered pectin
> ¼ cup cold water

Remove the pits and crush the fruit. If you want to peel the apricots (I never do), plunge the fruit in boiling water for 15 seconds and then put into cold water and peel. Add the sugar, corn syrup, and lemon juice. Mix well. Let the fruit stand for 30 minutes. Mix the pectin and cold water in a small pan until well blended. Bring to a full rolling boil and boil for 1 minute. Pour it into the fruit mixture and stir for 3 to 5 minutes. Ladle the jam into hot jars. Wipe the rims of the jars and seal. Let stand at room temperature for 24 hours, then freeze the jam for up to 1 year. Defrost in the refrigerator and keep unused jam in the refrigerator.

. . . .

BOURBON-SPIKED ASIAN PEAR JAM

Asian pears are a cross between apples and pears, and when ripe are juicy and luscious. Fresh currants are now available during midsummer in grocery stores. They look like beautiful, shimmering red rubies.

Makes about 5 half-pints

    4 cups peeled, cores removed, and chopped Asian pears
    2 cups fresh currants, carefully removed from stems (patience!)
    2 tablespoons orange juice
    1 tablespoon orange zest
    1 tablespoon finely chopped crystallized ginger
    ½ teaspoon cinnamon
    4½ cups brown sugar
    2 tablespoons bourbon

Put all of the ingredients, except the bourbon, into a heavy 4-quart pot and bring to a rolling boil, stirring to dissolve the sugar. Reduce the heat and cook until a temperature of 218–220°F is reached, about 20 minutes. Remove from heat and discard any foam that accumulates on the jam. Stir in the bourbon and let the jam rest for 5 minutes before ladling into jars and continuing as described on pages xvii–xviii.

CARROT—PINEAPPLE JAM

....

▣ *If you love carrot cake, try putting a teaspoon of Carrot—Pineapple Jam in the center of an oatmeal-raisin muffin before baking. When you bite into the muffin you will have a delightful surprise.*

Makes about 5 half-pints

> 2 cups cleaned and shredded carrots
> Two (8½ ounce) cans crushed pineapple, in heavy syrup
> 1 large pear, peeled, cored, and chopped
> 2 cups sugar
> 1 cup brown sugar
> 1 teaspoon cinnamon
> ½ teaspoon *each* ground cloves and nutmeg
> ¼ cup orange juice
> ½ teaspoon butter or margarine

Preheat the oven to 350°F. Put all of the ingredients, including the heavy syrup from the pineapple, into an oven-proof pan. Mix the ingredients until everything is blended. Place the pan in the oven and let the mixture cook for 30 minutes, stirring every 15 minutes. Reduce the oven temperature to 325°F and continue to cook until the mixture is slightly transparent and passes the plate test described on page xiv. Ladle into jars as directed on pages xvii–xviii.

....

FRANGELICO FIG JAM

....

▣ *This jam tastes fantastic on French toast or a large Dutch baby pancake, and slivering the peel of the orange makes a beautiful presentation.*

Makes 5 half-pints

> 2 cups peeled and mashed figs
> 2 cups chopped quince, peeled and cores removed
> 2 tablespoons orange slivers
> 2 cinnamon sticks
> ¼ cup orange juice concentrate
> 3 cups sugar
> 2 to 3 tablespoons Frangelico liqueur

Put all of the ingredients, except the liqueur, in a heavy pot and bring to a rolling boil, stirring constantly. Reduce the heat, cook, and continue stirring until the mixture is thickened and bright in color. Remember that the jam will become thicker as it cools. Discard cinnamon sticks. Skim off any foam and stir in the liqueur. Let the mixture sit for 5 minutes and then ladle into jars as described on pages xvii–xviii.

....

LEMONY PRUNE JAM

....

🔳 *Stirring some Lemony Prune Jam into your devil's food cake batter or brownie batter gives these desserts a nice moist taste.*

Makes about 4 half-pints

> 1 pound pitted prunes
> Water
> 2 lemons, washed, quartered, and sliced thin
> ¼ cup sugar
> ½ cup honey
> ½ teaspoon each ground cinnamon and cloves
> 2 tablespoons brandy

Put the prunes into a pan and cover with water. Cook for 15 to 20 minutes and drain, reserving ½ cup of the liquid. Chop the prunes finely and place them in a heavy pot. Add the lemons, sugar, honey, cinnamon, cloves, and reserved cooking liquid, and cook for 10 to 15 minutes or until the desired consistency has been achieved. Stir in the brandy, then let the jam sit for 5 minutes. Ladle into jars, following the directions on pages xvii–xviii.

....

MANGO MADNESS JAM

··

This mango jam is unbelievably good on grilled chicken or fish.

Makes 6 to 7 half-pints

   4 mangos, pits removed, peeled and diced (about 2½ cups)
   1 cup quartered strawberries, stems removed
   1 cup mashed banana (you'll need about three bananas)
   2 tablespoons orange juice
   3 tablespoons lemon juice
   4 cups sugar
   1½ teaspoons nutmeg
   2 tablespoons Jamaican rum

Put the mangos, strawberries, mashed banana, juices, sugar, and nutmeg into a heavy pot and mix well. On high heat, bring the mixture to a rolling boil, stirring constantly. Reduce the heat to medium high and continue to cook until the mixture turns transparent or reads 218°F on a thermometer. Remove from heat and skim off any foam. Stir in the rum and let the mixture sit for 5 minutes. Ladle into jars, following the directions on pages xvii–xviii.

··

NECTARINE AND BLUEBERRY JAM

··

Nectarine and Blueberry Jam is the most beautiful color. Try spreading this jam over a cheesecake so you can enjoy its gorgeous glow.

Makes 5 half-pints

    1 ½ cups fresh blueberries
    2 ½ cups peeled and chopped nectarines
    4 cups sugar
    2 tablespoons lemon juice

Put the blueberries, nectarines, sugar, and lemon juice in a heavy pan and bring to a boil, stirring until all of the sugar is dissolved. Let the mixture come to a boil. Reduce the heat slightly, keeping the jam at a gentle boil. Boil for 15 to 20 minutes, skimming foam from the top, until the jam reaches 218°F or passes the plate test (see page xiv). Remove from heat and let the mixture sit for 5 minutes. Ladle into hot jars and continue as directed on pages xvii–xviii.

OLLALABERRY JAM

Today we hear of many different types of berries, but sometimes have a difficult time finding them in our markets. The ollalaberry was developed as a superior variety of the boysenberry.

Makes about 4 half-pints

4 cups ollalaberries
2 tablespoons lemon juice
3 cups sugar
¼ cup crème de cassis

Wash and pick over the berries. Put all of the ingredients, except the crème de cassis, into a heavy pot and bring to a boil, stirring until the sugar dissolves. Reduce the heat and continue to cook until the jam becomes transparent and shiny, about 18 to 20 minutes or until a thermometer reads between 218 and 220°F. Remove from heat and skim off the foam. Stir in the crème de cassis, then let the mixture sit for 5 minutes before ladling into hot jars. Continue as directed on pages xvii–xviii.

. . . .

Papaya–Grapefruit Jam is wonderful spread lightly on a plain cake or as a thin layer on top of a white chocolate cheesecake.

Makes 5 to 6 half-pints

> 4 papayas, peeled, seeds removed, and diced (about 2½ cups)
> 3 large grapefruit, peeled, seeded, sectioned, and chopped
> 2½ cups sugar
> 2 tablespoons honey
> 2 tablespoons passion fruit liqueur or Triple Sec

Put the papayas, grapefruit, sugar, and honey into a large heavy pot and bring to a rolling boil, stirring to dissolve the sugar. Reduce the heat to medium high and continue to cook, stirring often, until the mixture turns transparent or reaches 218°F. Skim off any foam and stir in the liqueur. Ladle into hot jars and continue as directed on pages xvii–xviii.

....

These three flavors complement each other beautifully.

Makes 5 half-pints

>   3 cups peeled, pitted, and chopped peaches
>   1 cup blackberries
>   1 cup crushed pineapple, juice included
>   2 tablespoons lemon juice
>   3 ½ cups sugar

Put all of the ingredients into a heavy pan and stir constantly while bringing the mixture to a rolling boil. Reduce the heat. Boil gently and cook until the mixture thickens, stirring frequently. Skim off any foam. When the mixture reaches 218°F remove it from the stove. Let the jam sit for 5 minutes, skimming off foam as it rests. Ladle it into hot jars and continue as directed on pages xvii–xviii.

· ·

Make sure the peaches are firm, yet ripe enough to have that delicious peach aroma.

Makes about 7 to 8 half-pints

> 4 cups peeled, pits removed, and chopped peaches
> 1 cup maraschino cherry juice, from the cherries (reserve the cherries for
>   other uses)
> ¼ cup orange juice
> 1 (2 ounce) package dry pectin
> 5½ cups sugar

Put the peaches, maraschino cherry juice, orange juice, and pectin into a pan and cook, stirring, on high heat until the sugar is dissolved and the mixture comes to a boil. When the mixture reaches a rolling boil that cannot be stirred down, pour in the sugar and stir while returning the mixture to a rolling boil. At this point boil for exactly 4 minutes (or as directed on the package of pectin). Remove from heat and skim off any foam from the jam. Let it sit for 5 minutes and then ladle the jam into hot jars. Continue as described on pages xvii–xviii.

· ·

PERSIMMON AND PINEAPPLE JAM

I love the taste of a fully ripe persimmon, and Persimmon and Pineapple Jam brings that flavor to you year round.

Makes 6 to 7 half-pints

> 3 pounds persimmons, cut in half and pulp scooped out
> 2 cups crushed pineapple, in heavy syrup
> 3 cups sugar
> 1 vanilla bean, cut in half lengthwise

Preheat the oven to 325°F.

Put all of the ingredients, including the heavy syrup, into an oven-proof Dutch oven. Warm the Dutch oven on top of the stove until the sugar dissolves. *Do not let it boil,* or the persimmons will develop a bitter taste.

Transfer the Dutch oven to the oven and cook slowly until the mixture thickens and becomes glossy. Remember, the jam will thicken even more as it cools. When done, transfer the Dutch oven to a cutting board, or other protected surface, and scrape the inside of the vanilla bean into the mixture. Dispose of the outer part of the bean. Let the jam sit for 5 minutes, ladle it into hot jars, and continue as described on pages xvii–xviii.

....

▨ *When you have too many tomatoes, make Spicy Tomato Jam. It's terrific on grilled fish, in omelets, or on light, airy biscuits.*

Makes 4 half-pints

> 2 pounds tomatoes
> 1 serrano chili, minced
> 4 cups sugar
> ¼ cup lemon juice
> ½ cup minced fresh cilantro
> One (12 ounce) can tomato juice

Peel the tomatoes by dropping them into boiling water for 1 minute; remove them quickly and peel. Crush the tomatoes and put them into a Dutch oven or jelly pan and simmer for 10 minutes. Stir in the chili and sugar, blending well. Mix in the lemon juice, cilantro, and tomato juice. Bring the mixture to a boil and stir until the sugar dissolves completely. Boil gently for about 10 minutes or until the fruit becomes transparent. Remove from heat and cover the Dutch oven. Let it sit out overnight. The next day reheat the mixture and cook until the jam thickens. Ladle it into hot jars and continue as directed on pages xvii–xviii.

....

TOMATO AND RED PEPPER JAM

....

🔲 *Spread some Tomato and Red Pepper Jam on a toasted baguette and top with grilled vegetables, chicken, white fish, or thinly sliced beef for a delicious open-face sandwich.*

Makes 5 to 6 half-pints

> One (12 ounce) jar of fire-roasted red peppers, drained and chopped
> 2 pounds tomatoes, peeled and chopped
> ¼ cup lemon juice
> ¼ cup slivered basil
> 2 cloves garlic, minced
> 3 cups sugar

Put all of the ingredients into a pan and bring to a boil, stirring to dissolve the sugar. Turn the heat down and continue to cook until the tomatoes turn bright and transparent; about 15 to 20 minutes at a gentle boil. Remove the pan from the heat and let it stand overnight, covered. The next day put the *tomatoes,* not the liquid, into clean hot jars. Boil the liquid until it is thick, like honey. Pour it over the tomatoes. Seal the jars, and continue as described on pages xvii–xviii.

🔲 *Because the tomatoes were kept at room temperature overnight, process them in a water bath for 15 minutes.*

....

Jellies

JELLIES ARE bright, shimmering beauties made from fruit juice or other liquids such as wine or champagne. When making jelly you can crush and drain fresh fruit, or use frozen fruit, frozen juices, or bottled juices. Crush the fruit with a food processor, heavy spoon, or potato masher. It is helpful, after crushing some fruits, to sprinkle them with sugar and let them sit for about an hour. This will help to draw the juices from the fruit before you start. To drain the fruit, use a strainer lined with cheesecloth or a suspended jelly bag. If you dampen the jelly bag it will help the fruit drain faster. Make sure you never try to rush this process by squeezing the jelly bag, or you will end up with cloudy jelly. If I have an abundance of summer fruit, and not much time, I will strain the juice, and freeze it in milk cartons to make jelly at a more convenient time.

Once you have the juice you are ready to make jelly. Some people prefer firm jelly—one that cuts and holds its shape; I like mine to quiver slightly and have a little softness to it. You can vary the consistency of your jelly by using either the *short-boil* or *long-boil* method (see page xii for a description). After you have decided which method you will use (some recipes specify the method), you can begin.

In all of these recipes I direct you to bring the ingredients to a "rolling boil," that is, a boil that even when stirred will not stop boiling. It is very important when using pectin to have the liquid this hot.

In the jelly recipes I call for "dry pectin" or "liquid pectin." There are several kinds and sizes (1¾ ounce or 2 ounce) of dry pectin on the market. I have given directions for general use but it is a good idea to check the directions of the particular pectin you are using to determine how long you should boil the jelly (1 to 4 minutes) after adding the sugar.

I also never mention using paraffin as a sealing method for jelly. You can use it, but I think it is safer, cleaner, and easier to use metal lids. Paraffin, if not used cautiously, can be very dangerous, causing burns and fires that can be serious. *Never* melt paraffin over direct heat or in a microwave—you will have a fire. Also, *never* put water on a paraffin fire—instead, just cover the fire with a lid to smother it.

....

🔲 *Kiwi–Grape Jelly is plain, simple, and striking to look at. Serve it in a crystal jar so its beauty can shine through.*

Makes about 8 half-pint jars

> 3 pounds kiwi, peeled and chopped
> 2 cups white grape juice
> 7 cups sugar
> 3 ounces liquid pectin

Put the kiwi and grape juice into a pan and bring the mixture to a boil. Remove from heat and let the mixture sit, covered, for 30 to 40 minutes. Drip the mixture through a jelly bag or a strainer lined with cheesecloth. Measure out 4 cups of juice. Put the juice and sugar into a heavy pan and cook until the mixture comes to a rolling boil (that is, one that can't be stirred down). Add the pectin all at once, and continue stirring until the mixture returns to a rolling boil. Boil, stirring constantly, for exactly 1 minute. Remove from heat and skim away any foam that has accumulated on top. Ladle into hot jars and continue as directed on pages xvii–xviii.

....

BLUSHING PINK JELLY

・・

🔲 *Wine jellies are mild tasting with a delicate hue. They are great served with cream cheese and crackers, or spread on certain cheeses such as my favorites Brie, Camembert, and Saint André.*

Makes 4 half-pint jars

    1 cup rosé wine
    3⅓ cups sugar
    3 ounces liquid pectin

Mix the wine and sugar in a pan until the mixture is very hot but not boiling. Stir until all of the sugar is dissolved. Right before the mixture boils, quickly stir in the pectin. Remove the pan from the heat, and stir to blend for 2 to 3 minutes. Remove any foam that forms. Ladle the liquid into hot jars, clean the rims of the jars with a damp cloth, and seal with very hot lids. Screw on the metal bands and put in a draft-free place to let the jelly set. It may take 2 days to set properly, so place the jars where they don't need to be moved.

🔲 *Try making Champagne Jelly! Substitute champagne for rosé in the recipe for Blushing Pink Jelly. For best results, pick a really good champagne.*

・・

APPLE–JALAPEÑO JELLY

......:...

🔲 *I like to use Apple–Jalapeño Jelly spread on a whole Brie cheese, wrapped in pastry, and baked. It is exquisite.*

Makes about 7 to 8 half-pint jars

> 6 Washington Delicious apples, peeled and puréed
> 2 fresh jalapeño peppers, minced
> 3 cups cider vinegar
> Apple juice
> 7½ cups sugar
> One (3 ounce) package liquid pectin

Put the apples, peppers, and vinegar into a pan and bring the mixture to a boil. Reduce the heat and cook until the apples are very tender. Put the mixture into a jelly bag and let it drain. Measure the liquid and add apple juice to make 4 cups. Put the liquid into a heavy pan and stir in the sugar. Bring the mixture to a rolling boil, stirring constantly. Stir in the pectin, and bring the mixture back to a rolling boil, stirring all the time. Once the mixture returns to a rolling boil, boil for 1 minute more. Remove from heat and skim off any foam that has accumulated. Ladle the liquid into hot jars and continue as directed on pages xvii–xviii. Turn the jars upside down for 5 minutes and then return them to an upright position to continue cooling.

....

CALVADOS–APPLE CIDER JELLY

. . . .

▣ *Calvados is very expensive. If it is not within your budget, buy applejack brandy—it works just as well. I get my apple cider from an apple farm, and it is full of flavor but also full of sediment. It's best to strain such unprocessed cider through a jelly bag before beginning this recipe.*

Makes about 4 half-pints

    2 cups apple cider
    4 cups sugar
    2 tablespoons lemon juice
    1 teaspoon cinnamon
    3 ounces liquid pectin
    2 tablespoons Calvados (optional) or applejack brandy

Combine the cider, sugar, lemon juice, and cinnamon in a heavy pan. Bring the mixture to a rolling boil, stirring constantly. Add the pectin all at once and keep stirring until the mixture returns to a rolling boil. Now, while still stirring, boil for 1 minute. Then remove the pan from the heat and skim off all foam. Stir in the Calvados or applejack and ladle into hot jars. Continue as directed on pages xvii–xviii.

. . . .

....

Orange–Chive Jelly is delicious brushed on Cornish game hens, chicken, or pork roasts as they bake.

Makes about 5 half-pints

> 2 cups orange juice, no pulp
> 2 tablespoons dried chives
> 2 cups honey
> 2½ cups sugar
> 3 ounces liquid pectin

Put the orange juice, chives, honey, and sugar in a heavy pan and cook, stirring constantly, until all of the sugar is dissolved. Continue to cook until the mixture comes to a full rolling boil. Add the liquid pectin and bring the mixture back to a rolling boil, stirring constantly. Cook the mixture at a rolling boil for exactly 1 minute. Remove from heat and skim off any foam from the top of the jelly. Ladle into hot jars and continue as described on pages xvii–xviii.

....

CRANBERRY–LEMON JELLY

. . . .

▣ *Cranberry–Lemon Jelly is both tasty and beautiful.*

Makes about 4 half-pints

> 3 whole lemons, washed well in hot water
> 7 cups washed and picked over cranberries
> ¾ cup water
> 2 cups sugar
> 1 cup honey

Cut the lemons in half and slice thin. Put the lemons, cranberries, and water in a heavy pan and cook for 10 minutes, or until the fruit is very soft. Transfer the fruit from the pan to a jelly bag or strainer lined with cheesecloth. Let the fruit drain. When you have 4 cups of juice, return the juice to the heavy pan and add the sugar and honey. Bring the mixture to a boil, stirring continuously. Lower the heat and gently boil the mixture for 10 to 15 minutes. At this point begin testing the jelly by the plate or sheeting method (see pages xiii–xiv), or use a thermometer to determine when the mixture reaches 218°F. Skim off any foam as the jelly cooks. When done, remove the pan from heat and skim off any remaining foam. Ladle into hot jars and continue as directed on pages xvii–xviii.

. . . .

CURRANT AND QUINCE JELLY

....

Put a dab of this jelly in the center of thumbprint cookies next time you make some.

Makes about 4 half-pints

> 2 cups stemmed, washed, and crushed currants
> 6 cups peeled, cored, and chopped quince
> 4 cups water
> 2 cups juice from white grapefruit
> 1½ cups sugar
> 1½ cups honey
> 2 tablespoons crème de cassis (optional)

Put the currants and quince into a pan along with the water and grapefruit juice, and bring the mixture to a boil. Reduce the heat and cook at a gentle boil until the quince are tender (this could take from 20 to 30 minutes). Let the cooked mixture drain in a dampened jelly bag or a strainer lined with cheese-cloth. Measure out 4 cups of juice and put it in a heavy pot. Add the sugar and honey. Cook until the mixture thickens and registers about 218°F on a thermometer, skimming off any foam as it cooks. Remove from the heat and stir in the crème de cassis (if desired). Ladle into hot jars and continue as directed on pages xvii–xviii.

....

FIERY HOT JALAPEÑO JELLY

Fiery Hot Jalapeño Jelly is surely one of my very favorite condiments. I love it spread on crackers, or mixed with broth and wine for a great chicken sauce. Try mixing it with rice vinegar and sesame oil for a delicious dressing, or blend it with a little melted butter as a topping for your favorite fish. The uses for this jelly are endless—have fun with it!

Makes about 6 half-pints

> 3 red jalapeños, stems removed, chopped (much of the heat is in the seeds;
>   I leave them in—you decide)
> 2 green jalapeños, stems removed, chopped (see warning above)
> 3 cups rice vinegar
> Water
> One (2 ounce) package dry pectin
> 3 cups sugar
> 2 cups light corn syrup
> 1 small red jalapeño, seeded and minced fine
> 1 small green jalapeño, seeded and minced fine

Put the chopped jalapeños (3 red and 2 green) and rice vinegar in a pan and bring to a boil. Let the mixture sit in a covered jar overnight.

The next day, drain the mixture in a jelly bag or in a strainer lined with cheesecloth. Measure the juice and add enough water to make 4 cups. Put the pepper liquid into a heavy pan and mix with powdered pectin. Bring the mixture to a rolling boil, stirring constantly. Immediately add the sugar and corn syrup while stirring and return the pan to a rolling boil. Boil for only 1 minute. Remove the pan from the heat and skim off any foam. Stir in the tiny minced peppers and mix well. Ladle into hot jars to within ½ inch of the top of the jar. Clean the rim of each jar with a hot damp cloth and seal with a hot lid and screw-on band. The jars can now be inverted for 5 minutes. Next, turn them upright. After about 5 minutes, tip each jar back and forth once or twice; this helps suspend the peppers throughout the jelly.

GARLIC–PEPPER JELLY

Since grilled chicken sandwiches are all the rage, try spreading Garlic–Pepper Jelly on a toasted baguette piled with thinly sliced grilled chicken, sprinkled with toasted chopped walnuts and lots of slivered lettuce, and maybe a few slices of fresh avocado, for a really sensational creation.

Makes about 6 to 7 half-pints

> 30 cloves garlic, chopped
> 2 cups white wine vinegar
> 1 cup white grapefruit juice
> 2 tablespoons fresh thyme, lemon thyme, or oregano
> 1 tablespoon red pepper flakes
> 3 tablespoons minced yellow bell pepper
> 4 cups sugar
> 2 cups water
> 2 cups light corn syrup
> 6 ounces liquid pectin

Place the garlic, 1 tablespoon herb, and 1 teaspoon red pepper flakes in a pan with the vinegar and grapefruit juice. Bring to a boil. Transfer the entire mixture to a jar and cover, leaving at room temperature overnight.

The next day, drain the mixture through a jelly bag or a strainer lined with cheesecloth. Measure out 2 cups of the liquid; if there is more, reduce to make 2 cups—this will intensify the flavors. Add the rest of the red pepper flakes, the bell pepper, sugar, water, and corn syrup and bring to a rolling boil in a heavy pot. While stirring constantly (you should not be able to stir down the boil), add the liquid pectin all at once. Continue stirring and bring the mixture back to a rolling boil. Now, continue to stir while boiling for 1 full minute. Remove from heat and skim off any foam that has accumulated. Stir in the remaining herb and ladle into hot jars, leaving ½ inch of head space. Clean the rims of the jars and place a hot flat lid on each jar and secure with a screw-on band. Turn the jars upside down for 5 minutes. Return them to an upright position and continue to cool.

LEMON SUNSHINE JELLY

....

Lemon Sunshine Jelly is a beautiful color and looks lovely spread on top of your favorite cheesecake or on a wonderful wine cake.

Makes about 4 half-pints

> 1 cup strained lemon juice
> ¼ cup lemonade concentrate
> 1 cup lemon verbena leaves, stems torn off
> 1½ cups boiling water
> 4¼ cups sugar
> 2 drops of yellow food coloring (optional)
> 3 ounces liquid pectin

Strain the lemon juice until clear and mix with concentrate. Set aside.

Put the verbena leaves into a bowl and pour the boiling water over the leaves. Cover the bowl tightly with foil and let stand for 15 to 20 minutes. Strain the mixture and add the liquid to the lemonade mixture; put all into a heavy pan. Add the sugar and stir well. Bring the mixture to a rolling boil, stirring constantly. Stir in the coloring (if desired) and liquid pectin and continue to stir constantly until the mixture returns once more to a rolling boil. Boil for exactly 1 minute more. Remove from heat and skim off any foam. Ladle into hot jars and follow the directions on pages xvii–xviii to finish up.

....

RED CURRANT AND RASPBERRY JELLY

....

🏵 *Fresh currants look like beautiful little jewels. This is a delicious jelly to give as a gift because of its beauty and delightful taste.*

Makes about 5 half-pints

    4 cups fresh red currants, stems removed
    5 cups raspberries
    1 cup water
    2½ cups sugar
    ¾ cup honey
    2 tablespoons crème de cassis

Cook the currants and raspberries in 1 cup of water until soft, about 10 minutes at a gentle boil. Crush the fruit and put it in a jelly bag or cheesecloth-lined strainer; collect the juice dripping through. When you have 4 cups of juice, place the juice in a heavy pan and add the sugar and honey. Bring to a boil, stirring to dissolve the sugar. Reduce the heat and let the mixture cook for 10 to 15 minutes at a gentle boil and then begin testing the jelly by the plate test or sheeting method described on pages xiii–xiv. When done, remove the jelly from the heat and skim off any foam that has accumulated. Stir in the crème de cassis and ladle into jars as described on pages xvii–xviii.

....

MELON MELODY JELLY

....

Here is a delightful combination of summer flavors.

Makes about 8 half-pints

    2 cups diced honeydew melon
    2 cups diced cantaloupe
    2 cups diced casaba melon
    7 cups sugar
    1 teaspoon cardamom seed
    ¼ cup lemon juice
    One (6 ounce) package liquid pectin
    ½ cup slivered mint

Put the diced melon and 1 cup of the sugar into a bowl and toss. Refrigerate overnight.

Transfer the melon mixture to a heavy pan, add the cardamom seed and lemon juice, and bring to a boil. Remove from heat and put the fruit in a jelly bag or a strainer lined with cheesecloth. Let the mixture drain until you have

....

4 cups of melon juice. Add the rest of the sugar to the juice and bring to a rolling boil (one that cannot be stirred down), stirring constantly, in a heavy pan. When the mixture boils, add the liquid pectin all at once. Return the jelly to a rolling boil and cook for exactly 1 minute. Remove from heat and stir in the mint. Ladle into hot jars and continue as directed on pages xvii–xviii.

MINTY PINEAPPLE AND GUAVA JELLY

. . . .

🖾 *This is an intriguing jelly to serve with lamb or pork. When picking guavas for this jelly, look for the firmer ones.*

Amount varies depending on how much guava juice was attained and how much sugar was added

> ¼ cup chopped fresh mint leaves
> 2 pounds guavas, ends discarded, cut into ½-inch chunks
> 2 cups fresh or canned crushed pineapple, including liquid
> Water
> Sugar (amount varies; see below)
> 1 tablespoon crème de menthe

Put the mint leaves, guavas, and pineapple in a heavy pan, adding enough water to just barely cover the guavas. Let the mixture cook on low heat for about 10 to 12 minutes. Pour the mixture into a jelly bag or strainer with a few layers of cheesecloth and let the mixture drain. Measure the amount of juice you have and return it to the pan. Add ¾ to 1 cup sugar (your preference) for every cup of juice that you have. Bring the mixture to a rolling boil (one that cannot be stirred down), stirring constantly. Reduce the heat to a gentle boil and let the mixture cook, skimming off any foam, until the mixture reaches the jell point of 218–220°F or passes the sheeting method or plate test (see pages xiii–xiv). This takes about 15 minutes. Stir in the crème de menthe and ladle into hot jars. Proceed as described on pages xvii–xviii.

MUSCAT GRAPE JELLY

▣ *For this jelly you need a grape that has lots of flavor. My mother always used Muscat grapes because they have a very distinct flavor. Today the Muscat grape is a little difficult to find (they used to be available in all grocery stores). Try looking for them at farmers' markets; if you're unable to find Muscat grapes, substitute black Concord grapes with seeds.*

Makes 7 to 8 half-pint jars

    3½ pounds Muscat grapes
    ½ cup water
    1½ cups light corn syrup
    5½ cups sugar
    1 tablespoon lime zest
    6 ounces liquid pectin

Remove the grapes from their stems and, without removing any seeds, put the grapes in a pan with ½ cup of water. Bring this mixture to a boil and boil for 5 minutes. Crush the grapes with any remaining water and pour the mixture into a jelly bag or a cheesecloth-lined strainer; let the juice drain.

When you have 4 cups of juice, combine it with the corn syrup, sugar, and zest. Place the mixture in a heavy pan and bring it to a rolling boil (one that cannot be stirred down). Add the pectin, stirring constantly until a rolling boil has again been achieved, and then boil for 1 minute. Remove from the heat and discard any foam that has accumulated on top of the jelly. Ladle the jelly into hot jars and continue as described on pages xvii–xviii.

POMEGRANATE–KIWI JELLY

. . . .

Pomegranate–Kiwi Jelly was the very first jelly I ever made. It was such a beautiful color, and had such a delicate taste, that I really became hooked on homemade jams and jellies.

Makes about 6 half-pint jars

   2 cups pomegranate juice
   1½ cups kiwi juice
   ¼ cup lemon juice
   One (2 ounce) package dry pectin
   5 cups sugar

An easy way to remove the seeds is to cut the top and bottom off the pomegranate and score the skin lengthwise in about four places. Submerge the pomegranate in a bowl of water and break it in pieces, under water. Separate the seeds, under water, from the pulp and the seeds will fall to the bottom of the bowl, while the pulp and skin float to the top. Crush the pomegranate seeds with your food processor. After you have crushed the seeds, let the juice of both pomegranates and kiwi drip through a jelly bag or a sieve lined with cheesecloth. When you have 3½ cups of juice, put the juice, lemon juice, and pectin in a heavy pot and blend well. Bring the mixture to a boil, stirring constantly. When the jelly has reached a full rolling boil, add the sugar all at once and stir until the mixture returns to a full rolling boil. Once it returns to a full boil and cannot be stirred down, time for 2 minutes. Remove from the heat and skim off any foam. Ladle into hot jars and continue as directed on pages xvii–xviii.

STRAWBERRY–PINK GRAPEFRUIT JELLY

The grapefruit gives Strawberry–Pink Grapefruit Jelly a nice tang. I like to stir some of this into my waffle batter.

Makes about 7 half-pint jars

> 2 cups strawberry juice (you'll need about 8 cups of strawberries)
> 1 ¾ cups pink grapefruit concentrate
> 7 cups sugar
> 6 ounces liquid pectin

Wash and stem the strawberries. Crush the strawberries and let the fruit drip through a jelly bag or a cheesecloth-lined strainer. When you have 2 cups of strawberry juice combine the juice, pink grapefruit concentrate, and sugar and cook until the sugar dissolves. While stirring constantly, let the mixture come to a full rolling boil. Remove from heat and quickly stir in the liquid pectin. Immediately turn the heat to high and return the mixture to a full boil. Once it is boiling hard, boil for 1 minute more. Remove from the heat and skim off any foam that has accumulated on top of the jelly. Ladle into hot jars, leaving ½ inch head space, and continue as directed on pages xvii–xviii.

WATERMELON JELLY

....

This jelly is such a beautiful color. Stir in a few black watermelon seeds before ladling the new-made jelly into jars. They may be a nuisance, but with just a few your jar of watermelon jelly will be gorgeous! This is a softer jelly.

Makes 6 to 7 half-pint jars

    4 cups watermelon juice (about ½ of a large watermelon)
    6½ cups sugar
    ¼ cup lemon juice
    6 ounces liquid pectin

Cut up the watermelon and purée in a food processor. Drain the watermelon in a jelly bag until you have 4 cups of watermelon juice. Put the juice in a pan and stir in the sugar and lemon juice. Bring the mixture to a rolling boil and boil until the sugar is dissolved. Add the pectin and stir until the solution clears. Ladle into hot jars to within ½ inch of the top and continue as described on pages xvii–xviii. This jelly takes about 36 hours to jell completely, so put the jars someplace where they'll be undisturbed.

....

CHAPTER THREE

Preserves

PERFECT PRESERVES contain brightly colored fruit that glistens, making them completely irresistible. Preserves are made with large pieces of fruit, or even whole fruit that is suspended in the jar. You can use one, two, or as many combinations of fruit as you wish. The distinguishing trait of a preserve is the perfectly distributed fruit in the jar. This is accomplished by letting the mixture sit for five minutes after the preserve has reached 218–220°F. This cooling process helps to keep the fruit from rising to the top of the jar and the juice from settling at the base of the jar. After the preserve has cooled for five minutes, you can continue by stirring the mixture once or twice and then ladling into hot jars, leaving a half-inch of head space, cleaning the rim of the jar and sealing with a hot lid and then screw on the metal band.

APPLE–GOOSEBERRY PRESERVES

. . . .

▣ *The next time you make an apple pie, brush a few tablespoons of these preserves on the bottom of the crust before adding the apple mixture. If you don't have any gooseberries available, you can substitute blueberries, blackberries, or raspberries.*

Makes 5 to 6 half-pints

> 2 cups chopped Granny Smith apples
> 2 cups gooseberries
> 2 tablespoons lemon juice
> 2 ½ to 3 cups sugar

Peel and core the apples. Chop them fine, or crush them in a food processor. Add the apples and gooseberries to a jelly pan or Dutch oven and stir in the lemon juice and sugar; mix thoroughly. Bring to a rolling boil, stirring constantly. Reduce the heat to a gentle boil and let the mixture cook, stirring occasionally, until the preserves turn transparent or until a temperature of 218–220°F has been reached. Skim away any foam that rises to the top and let the mixture sit for 5 minutes before ladling into hot jars. Continue as directed on pages xvii–xviii.

. . . .

▣ *Chambord preserves are terrific when spread between layers of chocolate cake and chocolate mousse to make a marvelous torte.*

Makes 4 to 5 half-pints

> 3 cups red raspberries
> 1 cup peeled, pits removed, and diced peaches
> 2½ to 3 cups sugar
> 2 tablespoons lemon juice
> 2 tablespoons Chambord liqueur

Put all of the ingredients, except the Chambord, into a heavy jelly pan or Dutch oven. Bring to a rolling boil, stirring to dissolve the sugar. Lower the heat to a gentle boil, stirring occasionally and continue to cook until the mixture is transparent and has reached a temperature of 218–220°F. Remove from the heat, skimming off any foam, and let cool for 5 minutes. Ladle into hot jars and follow the directions on pages xvii–xviii to complete.

. . . .

CRANAPPLE PRESERVES

··

🔲 Remember to buy extra cranberries during the holiday season to use year around. Just leave them in their plastic bags—they freeze beautifully.

Makes 5 to 6 half-pints

> 3 cups fresh or frozen cranberries
> 2 cups peeled, cored, and chopped Granny Smith apples
> 1 whole lemon, washed, quartered, seeded, and sliced thinly
> 1 cinnamon stick
> ½ teaspoon nutmeg
> 3 cups sugar
> ½ cup light corn syrup

Put all of the ingredients into a heavy jelly pan or Dutch oven and bring to a rolling boil, stirring to dissolve the sugar. Lower the heat to a gentle boil and continue to cook until a temperature of 218–220°F, or the desired thickness has been reached. Remember, preserves will thicken as they cool. Remove from the heat and discard the cinnamon stick. Let the mixture sit for 5 minutes and skim any foam off the top before ladling into hot jars. Continue as directed on pages xvii–xviii.

··

FIG AND PINEAPPLE PRESERVES

....

▣ *I like to stir about ⅓ cup of these preserves into my homemade spice cakes.*

Makes about 6 half-pints

3 cups chopped fresh pineapple
2 cups chopped figs
¼ cup lemon juice
3½ to 4 cups sugar

Put the pineapple, figs, lemon juice, and sugar into a heavy pan and stir until the sugar dissolves. Bring the mixture to a rolling boil, stirring constantly. Reduce the heat and let the mixture slow-boil until thickened and the preserves reach a temperature of 218–220°F. When done, remove the preserves from the heat and skim off any foam that has accumulated on top. Let the mixture sit for 5 minutes and then ladle into hot jars. Continue as described on pages xvii–xviii.

....

. . . .

▣ *This is such a simple method of making preserves and provides great flavor. My mom used to make a quick pot of this kind of preserve with whatever fruit we had around.*

Makes 4 to 5 half-pints

> 4 cups blackberries
> 2½ to 3 cups sugar
> ¼ cup lemon juice

Crush the berries. Put the crushed berries, sugar, and lemon juice into a heavy pot and stir until the mixture comes to a rolling boil. Reduce the heat and cook until the fruit becomes transparent or until a temperature of 218–220°F has been reached. Remove from the heat and let the preserves sit for 5 minutes. Ladle into hot jars and continue as instructed on pages xvii–xviii.

GRANNY WALKER'S NECTARINE–APRICOT PRESERVES

....

I usually peel nectarines, but leave the skin on apricots. It's just a matter of preference.

Makes 7 to 8 half-pints

    3 pounds nectarines, peeled and chopped (you'll need 7 to 8 nectarines)
    3 pounds apricots, pits removed, chopped
    ¼ cup lemon juice
    1 tablespoon lemon zest
    4½ to 5 cups sugar
    2 tablespoons chopped crystallized ginger
    1 teaspoon cinnamon
    ½ teaspoon *each* nutmeg and ground cardamom

Put all of the ingredients into a heavy pot and mix well. Bring to a boil, stirring constantly, until all of the sugar dissolves. Reduce the heat and cook, skimming off any foam that accumulates, until the mixture is transparent and registers 218–220°F on a thermometer. When done, remove the preserves from the heat and skim off the rest of the foam. Let the mixture sit for 5 minutes, then ladle it into hot jars. Continue as directed on pages xvii–xviii.

....

GREEN PRESERVES

. . . .

📖 *Green Preserves can light your fire if you add a little more jalapeño.*

Makes 8 to 9 half-pints

> 8 tomatillos, papery skin removed, chopped (about 1 cup)
> 3 green peppers, seeds removed, chopped
> 2 zucchini, shredded
> 1 onion, chopped
> 2 jalapeños, minced
> ½ cup cider vinegar
> ⅓ cup chopped cilantro
> 7 cups sugar
> 3 ounces liquid pectin

Put the tomatillos, peppers, zucchini, onion, jalapeños, and vinegar in a heavy pan and cook uncovered on medium until the vegetables soften. Add the cilantro and sugar and mix well. Bring the mixture to a rolling boil (one that cannot be stirred down). Do not reduce the heat. While stirring constantly, boil for exactly 1 minute. Remove from the heat and stir in the liquid pectin. Stir well and skim any foam from the top of the preserves. Let the mixture sit for 5 minutes and then ladle into hot jars. Continue as described on pages xvii–xviii.

. . . .

. . . .

It intrigues me how wonderful tomato preserves are. I have canned tomatoes and tomato-based sauces for years, but was not interested in making tomato jams or preserves until recently, when I tried some and discovered how wonderful they are.

Makes 7 to 8 half-pints

> 2 pounds tomatoes (about 4 cups)
> 6 cups sugar
> ⅓ cup lemon juice concentrate
> 1 tablespoon lemon zest
> 6 ounces liquid pectin

Peel the tomatoes by dropping them in boiling water for 30 seconds. Take them out of the water and remove the peels–they will slide off easily. Crush the tomatoes and put them, along with the sugar, lemon juice concentrate, and zest, into a jelly pan or Dutch oven. Mix well and bring to a rolling boil, stirring constantly. Boil for 1 minute. Remove from the heat and stir in the pectin, stirring constantly for 1 minute more. Skim off any foam from the top and set aside for 5 minutes. Ladle into jars and continue as instructed on pages xvii–xviii.

. . . .

PERFECT PEACH PRESERVES

....

🁢 *Nature at its best is divinely preserved in this recipe. Use firm, ripe peaches rather than overripe peaches.*

Makes 5 to 6 half-pints

> 5 cups peeled, pitted, and chopped peaches
> 1 cup peach nectar
> 2 tablespoons lemon juice
> 4 cups sugar
> 1 teaspoon vanilla

Peel, pit, and chop the peaches. Blend the peaches with the nectar, lemon juice, and sugar and bring to a rolling boil in a heavy pot. Turn down the heat, and continue to cook over low heat, stirring occasionally. Skim away any foam that appears, until the mixture is transparent or registers 218–220°F on a thermometer. Remove from the heat and stir in the vanilla. Remove any remaining foam and let the mixture sit for 5 minutes, then ladle into hot jars following the instructions on pages xvii–xviii.

....

PLUM AND KUMQUAT PRESERVES

....

▣ *Kumquats are members of the citrus family. Pick firm, heavy-feeling fruit for best results.*

Makes 5 to 6 half-pints

> 1½ pounds kumquats
> 1½ pounds Damson plums
> 1 can mandarin oranges, drained and crushed
> 4½ cups sugar
> 1 teaspoon cinnamon
> ½ teaspoon allspice
> 2 tablespoons Triple Sec liqueur

Wash the kumquats and remove the stems. Prick each kumquat with a fork and drop into boiling water, cooking until tender (about 10 to 12 minutes). Drain the fruit, cut in half, and remove the seeds. Chop by hand or use your food processor.

Peel, remove pits, and chop the plums. Put the plums, kumquats, oranges, sugar, and spices into a heavy pot and cook, stirring occasionally, until the fruit is glossy or reaches a temperature of 218–220°F. Remove the pot from the heat and skim off any foam. Stir in the Triple Sec and let the mixture sit for 5 minutes. Ladle into hot jars and continue as described on pages xvii–xviii.

....

PEACH AND GRAND MARNIER PRESERVES

....

▣ *My parents loved to make preserves by slow-cooking a large amount of fruit in the oven for a long time. My dad knew exactly when they were done, just by looking at them. They were perfect every time.*

Makes 5 to 6 pints

    5 pounds peaches, peeled, pitted, and diced
    One (12 ounce) can crushed pineapple, in heavy syrup, undrained
    4 to 5 cups sugar
    ¼ cup lemon juice
    2 cinnamon sticks
    ½ teaspoon *each* cloves and nutmeg
    ¼ teaspoon mace
    2 tablespoons Grand Marnier

Preheat the oven to 325°F. Place the diced peaches, pineapple (with the syrup), sugar, lemon juice, cinnamon sticks, and spices in a heavy, oven-proof pan that can also be used on top of the stove. Put the mixture on top of the stove, on high heat, and stir to dissolve the sugar. Bring the mixture to a full rolling boil. Remove the pan from the heat and transfer it to the oven. Cook, stirring every 15 minutes, until the preserves are transparent and thickened, about 218–220°F for 1½–2 hours. Remove the preserves from the oven and skim off any foam that has formed on top. Discard the cinnamon sticks. Stir in the Grand Marnier and let sit for 5 minutes. Ladle into hot jars. Complete by following the directions on pages xvii–xviii.

SPICY BLUEBERRY–LEMON PRESERVES

....

🔖 *Spicy Blueberry–Lemon Preserves are perfect to use in crumb cookie bars, inside a puff pastry turnover, or inside a beautiful, sweet breakfast cake.*

Makes 5 to 6 half-pints

> 4 cups blueberries, picked over, any stems removed
> 2 whole lemons
> 2 tablespoons lemon juice
> ½ teaspoon *each* mace, cardamom, and nutmeg
> 2½ to 3 cups sugar

Prepare the blueberries and set aside.

Thoroughly wash the lemons. Cut into quarters, remove the seeds, and slice thinly.

Put all of the ingredients into a heavy pan and bring to a boil. Stir constantly until the fruit is at a full rolling boil. Reduce the heat and cook, stirring occasionally, until the mixture reaches a temperature of 218–220°F. Remove the pan from the heat and skim off any foam. Let the mixture sit for 5 minutes, then ladle into hot jars and continue as described on pages xvii–xviii.

....

STRAWBERRY–HONEYDEW PRESERVES

. . . .

🔲 *You can't really taste the honeydew in this recipe; it just lends a very interesting taste to the strawberries.*

Makes 5 to 6 half-pints

> 4 cups chopped strawberries
> 1 cup chopped honeydew melon
> 3 cups sugar
> ¼ cup orange juice

Put the strawberries and melon in a large pan. Mash the fruit slightly. Add the sugar and orange juice and mix well. Turn on the heat and stir until all of the sugar is dissolved. Bring the mixture to a boil. Reduce the heat and cook, stirring occasionally, for 15 to 20 minutes or until the preserves are of the desired thickness. Skim off any foam that accumulates while cooking. Remove the pan from the heat and let the preserves sit for 5 minutes before ladling into hot jars. Follow the instructions for sealing on pages xvii–xviii.

. . . .

STRAWBERRY–RHUBARB PRESERVES

. . . .

🏳 *Try spreading these preserves on the inside of a breakfast yeast cake before baking it.*

Makes about 6 to 7 half-pints

> 3 cups trimmed and thinly sliced rhubarb
> 1 cup water
> 3 cups crushed strawberries
> 1 tablespoon orange zest
> ½ teaspoon *each* nutmeg and allspice
> 1 cinnamon stick
> 4 cups sugar
> ½ teaspoon butter

Put the rhubarb and water in a pan and cook until the rhubarb is tender. Drain.

Combine the cooked rhubarb, strawberries, orange zest, spices, cinnamon stick, sugar, and butter, in a heavy pot and bring to a rolling boil, stirring constantly. Reduce the heat and continue cooking, stirring occasionally, until the mixture reaches a temperature of 218–220°F. Skim off any foam that accumulates. Remove the preserves from the heat, discard the cinnamon stick, and let sit for 5 minutes. Ladle into hot jars and continue as described on pages xvii–xviii.

. . . .

....

🔲 *These unusual preserves are delightful on cornbread.*

Makes about 6 to 7 half-pints

> 2 pounds yellow tomatoes (about 4 or 5 tomatoes)
> 2 zucchini, shredded
> 1 can crushed pineapple, include juice
> ¼ cup lemon juice
> ½ teaspoon turmeric
> ½ teaspoon *each* nutmeg, cinnamon, and cloves
> 4 cups sugar
> One (6 ounce) package lemon Jell-O

Peel and chop the tomatoes. Put the tomatoes, zucchini, pineapple, lemon juice, spices, and sugar in a heavy pan and bring to a rolling boil. Cook the mixture for about 10 minutes. Reduce the heat and cook until the preserves are of the desired thickness. Remove the pan from the heat and stir in the Jell-O thoroughly. Skim off any foam. Let the mixture sit for 5 minutes before ladling it into hot jars. Continue as described on pages xvii–xviii.

....

THREE-BERRY PRESERVES

....

🔲 *This recipe is a classic, full of nostalgia.*

Makes 5 half-pints

  1 cup strawberries
  2 cups blackberries
  1 cup raspberries
  2 tablespoons lemon juice
  3 cups sugar

Cut up the strawberries or crush with a few pulses in a food processor. Put all of the ingredients in a heavy pan and mix well, crushing all of the berries as you stir in the sugar. Turn on the heat and bring the mixture to a boil, stirring until all of the sugar dissolves. Cook the mixture at a gentle boil until it becomes translucent and reaches the desired thickness. Use a metal spoon to remove any foam that accumulates. Remove the pan from the heat and let the preserves sit for 5 minutes. Continue as described on pages xvii–xviii.

🔲 *For those of you who want seedless berry preserves, crush the berries together thoroughly. Press them through a mesh strainer and continue the recipe with the now-seedless pulp.*

....

Gift Wrapping

WHAT COULD be a more delightful gift than something that has been made and given from the heart? A beautiful basket full of delicious treats like jams, jellies, and preserves can be enjoyed in the heat of summer or on a rainy afternoon and bring a little sunshine back into your life.

After years of trying so hard to think of the perfect—yet inexpensive—gift to give to friends, neighbors, and co-workers, I came to the conclusion that the most appreciated and enjoyed gift was the one that was made by hand. Since my business is cooking, I chose to make gifts from my kitchen.

In this first book of the Good Gifts from the Home Series, I have made many different jams, jellies, and preserves. These jewel-like treasures are full of summer remembrances that bring cozy, warm feelings of caring to those who receive them.

Whether you are giving jams, jellies, or preserves to a new neighbor, or as a thank-you gift for a dinner or stay with friends, or as a Christmas or birthday gift, or for any special occasion, packaging these gifts can be fun and creative.

Label Your Jars

After you have made your gems you should label the jars, including the recipe name and the date that you made it. Most jams, jellies, and preserves, if kept in a dark, cool place, will last a year or more. Surely, given as a gift, they will be used long before that, but it is still a good idea to post the date on which the preserve was made. You can use self-adhesive canning labels (there are many beautiful ones to choose from in gift and card shops), or you can hang a label from the metal ring of the lid, using raffia, brown postal string, or thin streamers of colorful ribbon to attach the tags. To create hanging labels, cut sturdy bases from recycled heavyweight paper, textured paper, cardboard, or heavy brown paper. Next, you can cut colored paper into fruit shapes, such as apples, bananas, or strawberries, or make circles, stars, or oblong shapes, stick them on the base, and write your note. Decorative stamp and ink sets are sold that make interesting tags with fruit borders, some of the stamps print "From the kitchen of," leaving you room to write what you wish on the tag. If you are giving a gift in the fall or at Thanksgiving, spraying a maple leaf with gold paint, letting it dry, and carefully writing or painting the information on the leaf makes a beautiful presentation. Then, using a hole punch to make a hole in the leaf, insert brown postal string and hang the leaf from the metal ring on the jar.

Making the Presentation

Once the jars are labeled, the fun begins as you think of ways to present these gifts. While your gift is surely beautiful enough to give as is, you may want to add a special touch. For example, you could put jams, jellies, or preserves in a box with colored tissue paper, or line a basket with a pretty napkin and fill it with jams. Cellophane wrapped around preserves and tied with ribbons is also nice. You could fill a brown paper bag with jams and tie it closed with raffia or brown postal string, or fill burlap bags and then tie them with gingham ribbon. You could also make the jars look especially appealing by topping them with a lace- or gingham-trimmed jar topper. Jar toppers are pieces of fabric, cut with pinking shears, or trimmed with lace and bunched together with elastic or ribbon to fit neatly on the screw tops of your jars. Toppers are easy to make and can be found in many gift or kitchen shops (I found some really beautiful lace ones in France). Hanging a slice of dried lemon, orange, or apple or a few little dried hot chili peppers also gives a great country look to your jars.

Giving a jam and including its recipe and a few other recipes where the jam is an ingredient (in a glaze for baked ham, a favorite chocolate and raspberry brownie, or an oriental barbecue sauce) is a terrific idea.

If You Want Your
Gift to Be More Substantial

If you would like to expand the present a little more, you could actually make the recipe incorporating the jam, jelly, or preserve that you are giving. You can then put the jam (for example), the dessert treat, and the recipes for the jam and dessert inside a cute container. Making a fresh batch of scones or biscuits to accompany some preserves would also be a welcome treat. These items can all be packaged using inexpensive wrappings (as I mentioned earlier), or you can create a more extravagant gift by wrapping the items more elaborately. For example, you could put a jar of jam, a few crumpets, and some exotic tea into a teapot made of chicken wire. You can find all kinds of cute things made out of chicken wire—chickens, tea pots, boxes, and baskets—and all of them are welcome additions to anyone's kitchen. There are also beautiful boxes shaped like hearts, circles, and squares and covered in lovely wallpaper that make great containers. Or, just to keep things simple, you could use a square box filled with jams and jellies, surrounded with sparkling tissue paper (you could stencil the paper if so inclined), and all tied up with shimmering wire-edged ribbon.

If you would like your jam to be the central theme of a gift basket, complement it with other items such as biscuit cutters, decorative jam spoons, gourmet teas and a tea infuser, a whimsical tea pot, a tea pot cozy, a decorative or crystal jam jar, little heart-shaped coeurs molds, a gourmet coffee and coffee mug, or a package of scone or biscuit mix. Try giving some strawberry jam along with a pretty little strawberry plant in a nice ceramic pot.

Your jam, jelly, or preserve can also be part of a larger gift. A special jar of home-made jam goes well with a berry strainer with platter, a basket, a moss basket for the garden, a wooden basket or wooden heart-shaped bowl, a stoneware bread basket, a silver bread basket, a copper jelly pan, a decorative colander, or any other great basket. You can place the jam alongside a muffin tin, a cornbread mold, a Swedish pancake pan, or a fantastic crepe pan. Wrap any of these up in a colorful sheet of cellophane and tie it with pretty ribbons or raffia.

Remember: The Real Gift Is
Your Time and Thoughtfulness

All these suggestions are to help you make the most of your hard work and to make your gift something special and memorable. Because I have six children and lots of friends and relatives, buying gifts is a year-round chore. When I realized how much my loved ones enjoyed gifts I had made myself, I started looking forward to planning for coming events. We have now made it a tradition in our family for everyone to try to make at least one thing for someone. That gift is always the most cherished. Last year my son, T.J., made everyone in the family a box or a plaque (he's in junior high school, and is taking wood shop). His teacher, Mr. Youngblood, was a real help, and now ten of us will always fondly remember T.J.'s junior high school days.

However you decide to present your treasures, they will be enthusiastically appreciated by anyone knowing the time and love you have personally put into making each jewel-like jar of jam, jelly, or preserve. Enjoy!

INDEX

Salsas, Chutneys & Relishes

Linda Ferrari

Revealing the secrets of classic salsas, chutneys, and relishes, Linda Ferrari presents everyone's favorite recipes and a host of thoroughly modern recipes too. Ferrari also presents ways to personalize and decorate your homemade gifts with the distinct love and warmth of a bygone era. Includes recipes for Apple–Walnut Chutney, Festive Cranberry Relish, and Jicama and Chili Salsa.

Oils, Lotions & Other Luxuries

Kelly Reno

*W*hile the luxuries made from these recipes are tempting enough to keep, they are made with friends, family, and loved ones in mind. Kelly Reno includes ideas for gorgeous wraps, packaging, and presentation. Includes recipes for Five-Oil Massage Blend, Vanilla Body Lotion, Rose Bath Beads, and Herbs and Fruit Dusting Powder.

PRIMA PUBLISHING
P.O. Box 1260BK
Rocklin, CA 95677

USE YOUR VISA/MC AND ORDER BY PHONE **(916) 632-4400**
Monday–Friday 9 A.M.–4 P.M. PST

I'd like to order copies of the following titles:

Quantity	Title	Amount
_____	*Jams, Jellies & Preserves* $12	_____
_____	*Salsas, Chutneys & Relishes* $12	_____
_____	*Oils, Lotions & Other Luxuries* $12	_____
_____	*Soaps, Shampoos & Other Suds* $12	_____
	Subtotal	_____
	Postage & Handling ($5 for first book, $.50 for additional books)	_____
	7.25% Sales Tax (CA)	_____
	5% Sales Tax (IN and MD)	_____
	8.25% Sales Tax (TN)	_____
	TOTAL (U.S. funds only)	_____

Hawaii, Canada, Foreign, and Priority Request orders, please call 632-4400

Check enclosed for $_____ (payable to Prima Publishing)
Charge my ❑ MasterCard ❑ Visa
Account No. _____   Exp. Date _____
Signature _____
Your Name _____
Address _____
City/State/Zip _____ Daytime Telephone (___) _____